Presbyopia
(Selected Poems)

By Allan Cameron

In which a befuddled and bespectacled poet, who can only focus on things afar, takes it upon himself to challenge the myopic trend that for more than two hundred years has both freed and entrapped our poets' minds, and in which he chooses to discourse, digress and aimlessly pontificate upon the nature of poesy both myopic and presbyopic while closed within the moment and the narrow confines of his dusty and chaotic study.

Vagabond Voices
Sulaisiadar 'san Rudha

© Allan Cameron 2009

First published in September 2009 by
Vagabond Voices Publishing Ltd.
3 Sulaisiadar
An Rubha
Eilean Leòdhais / Isle of Lewis
Alba / Scotland HS2 0PU

ISBN 978-0-9560560-3-0

The author's right to be identified as author of this book under the Copyright, Designs and Patents Act 1988 has been asserted.

Printed and bound by Thomson Litho, East Kilbride

For further information on Vagabond Voices, see the website:
www.vagabondvoices.co.uk

In memory of my father who instilled in me a love of poetry by reciting it when he was drunk – that's the manner in which it should be treated. He mocked pretentious poets and savoured the poetry for what it was for him: sound and significance that reassured through its familiarity.

Contents

Introductory Essay on Presbyopia   i-xxx

Presbyopia   1

Auto-da-fé (or How I burnt a planet at the stake)   2

Rebirth of the gods   3

The loser   6

Jan Paweł   7

Lines scribbled on hearing ...   8

Have I not finished yet?   9

Utilitarianism   10

Elegy for Orwell   11

The emperor hack   14

Empire   16

Progress   17

State-indoctrinated doggerel   18

The second telling   19

Captain R and the culture of impunity   21

Un eroe del nostro tempo   24

A hero of our time   25

Untitled poem and translation   26

Matter that little matters ...   27

I took the puzzle down ...   28

The North Sea   29

Hope and the red hero   30

Religion   31

Poets without passion   32

Reflections on being told that Gaels ...   33

Zarathustra's last interview   35

Fascism encountered in a city park   41

The well-drop drew ...   42

You are either with us or against
us in the clash of civilisations   43

The moment   44

Prayer to the muse   45

A joyous solitude   46

Europe   49

Europa   50

Europe, my love   51

Europe, you killed ...   52

La letteratura   55

Sotto la statale   56

Se oggi il sole non splende ...   57

Quelle sere   58

L'uomo solitario   60

Una donna   61

Come dobbiamo pesare ...   62

In cerca del canto   64

La torre d'avorio   66

Il riflusso   67

Ancora riflusso   68

A touch of myopia   69

Vagabond Voices is indebted to the Italian Institute of Culture in Scotland for its assistance in launching this collection of English and Italian poems.

The author wishes to thank the Scuola Normale Superiore di Pisa for the hospitality it provided in order that he could work on this and other texts in the autumn of 2008.

Presbyopia
(Greek: presbys, 'old', + ops, opos, 'eye')

*Daltonici, presbiti, mendicanti di vista
il mercante di luce, il vostro oculista,
ora vuole soltanto clienti speciali
che non sanno che farne di occhi normali.*

*Non più ottico ma spacciatore di lenti
per improvvisare occhi contenti,
perché le pupille abituate a copiare
inventino i mondi sui quali guardare.*
(Fabrizio de André, *Un ottico*)

"Cha tig an aois leatha fhèin" is sometimes accompanied by the speaker tapping his hand against his malfunctioning or rheumatic leg. It means that old age does not come on its own, and like any other expression in a human language, it defies satisfactory translation into any of the other six thousand odd languages that still happily crowd this planet, although for how long we do not know. In Gaelic it invites the other person's ritual reinforcement of this self-evident truth, "Cha tig!" – a response that is possibly accompanied by indicating some other ailing part of the body. But age does not just bring physical afflictions: it brings a detachment, a distance from one's own birth and therefore a distance from the youthful self whose essence was made up of hopes, ambitions and a fond belief in certainties. In later years, no pleasure can be enjoyed with the same intensity and no fear can induce the same terror. But at the same time, a person who has read a few books and studied past reflections on the past will become increasingly aware of how he or she belongs not to one generation – to a period of time that has gathered its strength like a wave approaching the beach before crashing and dissipating its forces in the shallows – but to all times that are battered by the same endless succession of waves. Old age meditates on the cyclical, while youth dreams of progress and, in its more passionate incarnations, of utopias.

The eye, which links us not only to a coloured image of our surrounding reality but also to its depth of field or distance, suffers from two very different defects: myopia and presbyopia. Myopia only afflicts some people and it afflicts them from their youth. They see what is close to them, but the distance remains blurred and unreachable. Presbyopia afflicts us in later life, and particularly those whose eyesight has hitherto been good. It makes it difficult to focus on what is close to our "self", but retains clarity for distant objects. These restrictions on our ability to perceive are reflected in the way we write and possibly in the way we live and think. In their extremes, they are not beautiful, particularly if we consider them in their non-literary context. A person who can only think about himself and his immediate surroundings is rightly accused of egotism, and a more improbable person who weeps for the victims of the Black Death while failing to be moved by the loss of a favourite uncle, childhood friend or, to be even more extreme, his own leg is rightly accused of perverse detachment, a questionable credibility and a possible love of histrionics and intellectual posturing. These emotional and cerebral perspectives, which I have called myopia and presbyopia by analogy with our sense of sight, may be defects in our everyday existence but they are not necessarily so in literature: they only become defects when they remain unchallenged for too long.

The long season of the myopic started with the Romantics. Seamus Heaney has described Wordsworth as "an indispensable figure in the evolution of modern writing, a finder and keeper of the self-as-subject".[1] As every literary movement comes into existence in opposition to what came before but also carries over what came before into the substance of its exciting change (particularly when it is most successful), the Romantics do not appear to be as dramatic a change to us now as they must have done at the time. Nor can we stop others from objecting that the myopic could be traced back to John Donne or even further, to Petrarch and beyond, because their arguments would not be without merit.[2] In literature and poetry, as in so many other things, there are short cycles and long cycles. The artist as individual came from far off, but at some stage he became just artist, self, self-expression, and self-obsession that has lost self-obsession's once great virtue: sincerity.

In literature, this development took a very different form from the other arts, because of its two very distinctive features: its reliance on two enormous technological developments and its lack of universality (it is only universal to its own language community).[3] The first change, writing, caused a shift from communal literary production to individual literary production (I argue that literature predates writing in

---

1. Seamus Heaney, "The Triumph of the Spirit", *The Guardian Saturday Review*, 11 February 2006, p. 21.
2. And of course you could go even further back. In his *Black Sea*, Neil Ascherson to some extent defends Ovid's *Tristia* against the complaint that it is "absurd, a wail of self-pity and self-obsession". He also quotes Konstantin Paustovsky's complaint that he "could never understand why the Black Sea had struck [Ovid] as gloomy. I had always thought of it as one of the brightest and gayest of seas." This is an aspect of extreme myopia: reality is imperiously altered to match the poet's mood.
3. I examine this argument in greater depth in my book on language, *In Praise of the Garrulous* (Sulaisiadar: Vagabond Voices, 2008), particularly pp. 73-93.

spite of any etymological objections, and even in fairly recent times, great literature has been produced by the illiterate). The memory became much less important, and the continuous editing and adaptation by successive generations *in their minds* disappeared for as long as the original manuscript survived. In other words, writing brought about the immutable text. The second technological change, printing, caused another shift with even more complex and contradictory results. The redundancy of memory was again increased. On the one hand, writing became more democratic because of its greater accessibility and presence, but as with all things democratic, it invited interference by the powerful (no longer being the privileged sphere of the powerful or servants of the powerful). The first index of prohibited books was written in the 1560s, and censorship became a profession. The two hacks were born: one was the brilliantly shifty juggler of words, the irreverent debunker and demystifier; the other was his usually less brilliant cousin, who made up for his not entirely indifferent ability with words by putting them to work for the powerful. Thus products of incredibly fertile imaginations struggled to provide a living for busy, crowded and often makeshift printers' workshops, while Aretino, a now little known sixteenth-century Italian poet, playwright and pornographer was feted by emperors and popes. Charles V gave him a gold necklace of tongues protruding through lips in a rude gesture (*linguacce*) – a reference to his trade as satirist using language (*lingua*, also "tongue") to attack the powerful usually in the pay of other powerful figures. The word had become a potent force outside religion.

But the real revolution comes, as Heaney suggests, with the Romantics (perhaps not greater than the previous ones, but the more stunning because it was not related to technological changes within the world of language). Written literature moved towards the people, and in so doing destroyed the residual brilliance of their oral literature and song. To some extent, Romanticism represented the rise of the individual and the mummification of the oral and popular tradition. However my intention is not to belittle the Romantic poets: their use of popular traditions was original and dramatic; it was also inevitable and necessary, because something at least was retained. I think that Shelley and Coleridge are among the great poets of our English language along with others, including obviously Shakespeare and Milton (but everyone must make their own list). And if I may be allowed a myopic aside, my father continuously recited Coleridge and Fitzgerald's *Omar Khayyám*. For me therefore that hauntingly beautiful narrative poem, *The Ancient Mariner*, is not just the wonderfully complex account of sin, pointless unconscious sin, and suffering that redeems through the consciousness it brings; it is also the expression of the delightful idiosyncrasy displayed by someone close to me whom I can only know now through memory. Of course, Coleridge was not myopic. He was not at all myopic. Nor was Shelley always myopic.

> *I met a traveller from an antique land*
> *Who said: Two vast and trunkless legs of stone*
> *Stand in the desert ... Near them, on the sand,*
> *Half sunk, a shattered visage lies, whose frown,*
> *And wrinkled lip, and sneer of cold command,*
> *Tell that its sculptor well those passions read*
> *Which yet survive, stamped on these lifeless things,*
> *The hand that mocked them, and the heart that fed:*
> *And on the pedestal these words appear:*
> *"My name is Ozymandias, king of kings:*
> *Look on my works, ye Mighty and despair!"*
> *Nothing beside remains. Round the decay*
> *Of that colossal wreck, boundless and bare*
> *The lone and level sands stretch far away.*

Shelley's short masterpiece, which must be seen as a complex work and not simply the homily on time and power beloved of schoolteachers, is perfect in form, sound and density of meaning. It is also extremely presbyopic. It starts with first-person narration (one indicator of myopia), but that is only in order to emphasise the distance between the poet-narrator and the description. The narration is in fact immediately halted and the "traveller from an antique land" is immediately brought to the forefront. At the time Shelley was writing, "antique" was perhaps taking on its modern meanings of outdated or even valuable through being old, while its previous meanings of "ancient" or simply "old" were disappearing. As with all good poetry the many meanings of the word tend to blend without any forced or laboured attempt at contradiction. The land is not only ancient in its existence and traditions, but also in its artefacts. It is a nation of decayed greatness.[4] We have moved over geographical distance to an unspecified desert land and back over temporal distance to the antiquity the West has always deified, particularly in the Modern Era. The poem has also shifted from narration to description. In fact the poet-narrator's only action is to meet the traveller. We are now introduced to the two main characters in the poem, the sculptor and the sculpted image of a man who called himself "the king of kings". The artist was brilliant, and yet his work is lifeless. Why? Not surely because it is inanimate, because it was always that. Possibly because nothing of the great panoply of power remains to give the statue meaning and therefore life, or possibly because

---

4. Amitav Ghosh was obviously drawn to this element when he entitled his magnificently interwoven personal diary and historical account *In an Antique Land* (London: Granta Books, 1998). This work could be described as a blend of the myopic and the presbyopic, although the diary says little about the author and his feelings, and generally retains a descriptive tone.

the skilled artist, in spite of his clever reproduction of the grimace of power, had produced something that was already dead as a result of his having subjugated his skill to the will of a tyrant. Then the chronological distance is emphasised by Ozymandius' vainglorious words as they were chiselled and recorded by the sculptor. They are ridiculed by the empty landscape. The presbyopic poet focuses on the far distance and the detachment is total. From this perspective the conceits of power are even starker. But it is not only the death of power that is described in this poem; there is also the death of art, which has its own conceits.

Shelley's *Stanzas Written in Dejection, Near Naples* is pure myopia. The poem is a description of beautiful surroundings that contrast with the anguished self. The start is fairly promising:

> *Like many a voice of one delight,*
> *The winds, the birds, the ocean floods,*
> *The City's voice itself, is soft like solitude's.*

But from the third stanza the poet launches wholly into his protestations of misery, which frankly are entirely lacking in depth.

> *Alas! I have nor hope nor health,*
> *Nor peace within nor calm around,*
> *Nor that content surpassing wealth*
> *The sage in meditation found,*
> *And walked with inward glory crowned –*
> *Nor fame, nor power, nor love, nor leisure.*
> *Others I see whom these surround –*
> *Smiling they live, and call life pleasure; –*
> *To me that cup has been dealt in another measure.*

The probably unintentional truth that lies in this poem is that the invention of individuality opens up the frightening and corrosive idea that everyone else is so much better at dealing with life. Of course, individualism was always there in human nature, at least in latent form, but it was new in literature and this anguished poet of the early nineteenth century would return, following the relatively brief season of presbyopic realism, in the form of the "inept", the completely alienated first-person narrator who populated early twentieth-century novels in tragic or comic form (the most famous example of its comic form did not appear in literature but in cinema, and was of course Charlie Chaplin). In this poetry, the individual became the centre of pressing emotional and material needs. Long gone is the Platonic disdain for pleasures, which was based not so much on their moral depravity as on the insatiability of the desires they engender.

After the Romantics, Freud also played a major part in the rise of the myopic, although I am not certain the Victorian gentleman entirely approved of it, as he agonised over the demise of civilisation. In many ways, Freud was a literary-philosophical figure like Plato. He dealt in wonderful and imaginative speculations. That does not mean we should ignore them, but we should not pretend that they were based on scientific method. Although the method was very similar to Plato's, the results of Freud's speculations were very different. While Plato advised against giving in to one's physical desires as they only become more powerful and take away all our useful time, Freud argued that we have to give in to our drives if we are to live a happy and full life. Thankfully I don't have to answer that question – or at least not here. Given the speculative but nevertheless not unconvincing nature of both sides of the argument, I suspect that we answer this question according to our own inclinations, which in turn are probably governed by our own age. Freud may seem more attractive in our youth and Plato in our mature years. Perhaps the answer could only be found by writing a Platonic dialogue in which Freud and Plato are the principal speakers.

One result of Freud's influence was the stunningly innovative novel by Italo Svevo: *The Confessions of Zeno*. The Italian writer, who for most of his life was a citizen of the Austro-Hungarian Empire, adopted a sceptical approach to psychoanalysis, and quipped that it was more useful to novelists than to the mentally ill. He claimed that we know little about ourselves, but ourselves are the thing we know most about. It is logical then to start with oneself. Svevo had discovered, as I'm sure many had before him, that self-obsession is completely transformed when it is fused with self-deprecation. However the self is a limited universe, and some writers wish to escape from it. Escape from it is for some writers the only way they can calm the anguish that the myopic feel they have to shout about. The feeling the presbyopic writer has when he focuses on a distant horizon may well be an illusion, not because of some absurd solipsistic argument, but simply because there are so many forces out there, so many imponderables, that even the most rational mind can never fully grasp them or the reality they produce. But that relativity of truth in literature is perhaps an affirmation of truth in the reality we experience.

In his acceptance speech for the Nobel Prize, Harold Pinter made the all-important distinction between the writer and the citizen.

> In 1958 I wrote the following: "There are no hard distinctions between what is real and what is unreal, nor between what is true and what is false; it can be both true and false." I believe that these assertions still make sense and do still apply to the exploration of reality through art. So as a writer I stand by them

but as a citizen I cannot. As a citizen I must ask: What is true? What is false?[5]

For writers to get out amongst the relative truths that eventually help us create an idea of the truth, however unfocused, they have to indulge in the presbyopic to a greater or lesser extent. Pinter's independent political stance is a reminder that writers are not only artists but also what he calls "citizens", by which I assume he means morally active individuals operating within a society with its own social morality, and therefore constantly having to renegotiate the mutual relationship between those two moralities. All good artists wish to defy their society's morality and to influence it at the same time. This quixotic act is rarely successful in the short term, but can be in the long term, although such success is often damaging to the work of art in itself, and if the artist is still alive, to the artist too, as in the case of Wordsworth.

I started to consider the problem of myopia and presbyopia when the idea of a collection of my poetry first came up. I write poetry not to express my feelings but to illustrate something that is distant from me, often things I disapprove of, such as Utilitarianism (p. 10), our treatment of our planet (p. 2) or a certain media magnate (p. 14). On occasions I describe abstractions I admire or at least have sympathy for in their absurdity, such as youth (p. 24-25), religious sentiment (p. 31) and egalitarianism (p. 30). One poem concerns that oldest of old chestnuts (or in literary terminology, *loci communes* or *topoi*): death (p. 29).[6] When I use the first-person, the "I" is actually a "we", as in the harangue against my generation (p. 2) or my examination of the artificiality of literature (p. 55). I

---

5. Harold Pinter, "Pinter v the US", *The Guardian G2*, 8 September 2005, p. 9.
6. In English, we lack a proper term for *topos*, because "commonplace" has been hijacked for another meaning.

have always felt that this kind of poetry has little chance of being listened to in the contemporary West – perhaps I should say the Anglophone West. Amongst the rejections of my novel, *The Golden Menagerie*, I have a splendidly dismissive and didactic one from a small and innovative publisher explaining why I would have "a hard time" publishing my "poetry" and "poetic prose" on philosophical thought. Then the editor was generously forthright in her analysis, something that is so much better than the polite platitudes publishers understandably feel they need to write (understandably, because they are motivated by the kindly desire not to discourage the rejected applicant): "I thought that what you have done may be useful as an intellectual exercise but poetry's appeal in the contemporary world is a lyric one and has little to do with the dense and abstract prose of political philosophy." For a moment, I could not understand what she meant, and my book and its introductory poems to each chapter were certainly not exclusively about politics. It gradually dawned on me that the key word was "lyric". My poetry did not come from the heart or, as I would prefer to define it, the self. And such poetry has no place in contemporary literature, in accordance with evolution of "the self-as-subject". The editor also claimed that my writing is inaccessible, although I find that criticism harder to understand, as it is the myopic that is difficult to access, because it assumes a unique viewpoint belonging to the poet or perhaps even a small intellectual clique. The myopic has accustomed us to obscurantism, whereas even the most complex of presbyopic poetry remains fundamentally accessible to anyone who wishes to make the effort.

Indeed the poetry of the twentieth century has often been an exercise in obscurantism, not without some exceptional results, but often teetering on the indecipherable. During the century that has just come to a close, myopia did not simply dominate poetry; at times it became poetry to the exclusion of all else. In 1930s Italy, a successful poetical movement boasted a rather intimidating name of *ermetismo* (Hermeticism), which clearly wanted to identify itself with the esotericism of Hermes Trismegistos (the Hermetic writings were Greek Neo-Platonic texts dating from a few centuries after Christ and produced in Egypt; they exemplify the arcane). This poetry, like the prose influenced by it, considered obscurantism to be a virtue, and was one of the most extreme movements away from the accessibility of nineteenth-century European literature (it was the most complete expression of this trend which had already commenced in the late nineteenth century with the advent of Decadentism). The poets of this "hermetic" movement, who included such famous names as Ungaretti and Quasimodo, later defended their stance by claiming that Fascism left them no choice but to retire into their ultra-myopic exclusivity. At times, theirs was poetry that questioned the need for a reader.

In post-war Italy, there was a reaction against this and the presbyopic returned in a manner that has never occurred in Britain, although it is quite possible that we will shortly be in for another reversal, with Italy (and perhaps other neo-Latin countries) shifting towards the myopic and Britain (and other English-speaking countries) shifting at least to some degree towards the presbyopic. But the fact is that the myopic always risks the exclusion of most readers by its adoption of a very specific viewpoint. In literature the authorial viewpoint always differs radically, but the horizon is always the same.

At this stage, I need to illustrate more clearly the difference between myopia and presbyopia in poetry and in literature in general. The best way to do so is with the table below:

Myopia	*Presbyopia*
Self	Suppression of self
Us	The others
Here	The horizon
Now	The past and the future
The contingent	The universal
The domestic	The social
Irrationalism	Rationalism
Emotion	Detachment
Desire	Idea
Certainty	Doubt
Monologue	Dialogue
Description	Narration
Present-tense narration	Past-tense narration
First-person narration	Third-person narration
Experience of life	Experience of ideas
Self-deprecation	Satire
Self-justification	Encomium
Self-expression	Form / rhetoric
Esoteric	Exoteric
Exclusivism	Openness
Romanticism	Classicism
Dionysianism	Apollonianism
Cavalcante	*Farinata*

Clearly no one can write by numbers, and no one is obliged to tick all the boxes on one side or other of this table. The instruments on both sides should be used in good writing; the argument here is that for some time we have tended to ignore the right-hand column. The fundamental dichotomy is the one between the "Self" and the "Suppression of the self", and from that certain other tendencies appear to flow. For instance, narration is more presbyopic than description. Narration forces the poet to go outside himself and create characters, as in a great poem I have recently discovered, Kipling's "Mary Gloster". This long narrative poem is written with such honesty and artistic integrity that it is both a tragic representation and a critique of imperialist capitalism in its initial and most adventurous stage, in spite of the writer's actual views. The narration took hold of Kipling and carried him where he probably did not want to go. Description is very often the physical and non-human environment that surrounds the self and in which the self can be reflected (either by its similarity to the poet's mood or by its contrasts with it). However, I have already shown that Shelley's presbyopic *Ozymandias* was predominantly a descriptive poem. Where there is myopic narration, it is more likely to be in the first person and the present tense.

Most importantly, the myopic tends towards certainty because the self is the dictator of its own small universe, but outside the self, the writer has to negotiate between different certainties. Once the writer creates genuinely autonomous characters that are not caricatures, then their various certainties and doubts should deprive the poem or novel of its own absolute certainty.

The distinction that will not be clear to most is the one between Farinata and Cavalcante, two characters from the tenth canto of Dante's *Inferno*. When a poet discovers Dante, he discovers his own inadequacy to the task ahead. T.S. Eliot defined him as at least as great as Shakespeare, and he also understood that unlike Shakespeare, Dante cannot be translated. Shakespeare is a very great presbyopic poet, so presbyopic that we don't really know who he is, and perhaps don't need to. It does not matter to our understanding of the poetry whether Shakespeare's works were in fact written by Francis Bacon, John Florio or any of the other contenders for his pen. It does not matter so much whether or not he was a Catholic. Shakespeare is so presbyopic that he becomes a nobody entirely obliterated by the power of his own work (I should clarify here that there is plenty of bad or mediocre presbyopic poetry which equally obliterates its authors, but in the case of Shakespeare, the greatness of the poetry somehow makes the insignificance of the poet all the more surprising; the sonnets are an exception to this argument, and more biographical information would certainly be useful here). Dante on the other hand is so overwhelming because he is utterly myopic and utterly presbyopic. And because of that powerfully myopic dimension to his poetry, the biographical information we do possess does help us to understand his work, but more information would be useful. Dante really does tick every box on both those lists: he is full of self-justification, he uses the universe and God to settle some personal accounts, he bares his parochial prejudices, he builds his universal political project and he indulges in endless encomia of those historical figures he has decided to like. He ranges over time and over real and imagined space. His description is so plastic that artists and sculptors have always been fascinated by him (most interesting are Rodin's sketches for statues he sadly never sculpted); his narrative is spellbinding and remains as fresh on the tenth reading as it does on the first. All is structured within the great architectures of his three canticles. This great soupy mixture should not work, but it does, it does, it does. It works so perfectly that it takes away the breath and the will to write. Prissy and arrogant Petrarch laughed at Dante's vast vocabulary and its coarse, unpoetic words (much as the eighteenth century took a slightly jaundiced view of Shakespeare). The idea that Dante claimed a privileged relationship with Virgil must have appeared ridiculous, because Petrarch had genuinely started the movement back to classical Latin and away from its medieval version. And long before Wordsworth, it was perhaps he who took the first tentative steps towards the poet as a special person and "the self-as-subject". Dante was self-obsessed, but as a politician and not as a poet. Dante's faults should be as dear to us as his merits, because he embraced everything with the erratic rationalism of the medieval mind that we find so hard to understand. Dante also coincidentally invented these two characters who perfectly symbolise the myopic and the presbyopic.

Cavalcante is the father of Guido Cavalcanti, a fellow poet of Dante's and like Dante an ardent supporter of the White Guelphs. Farinata is a powerful Ghibelline warlord and Florentine patriot, whom Dante admires in spite of his different political allegiance.[7] The poet encounters them in the circle of hell reserved for the "Epicureans" or heretics who did not believe in the immortality of the soul when they were alive. As usual Dante describes the scene, narrates the encounter and uses Virgil to expatiate on the religious doctrine.[8] This is a silent and desolate area of hell, a kind of graveyard, but the graves are all open awaiting

---

7. In reality, the White Guelphs, with their pro-imperial line, had almost become a replacement for the Ghibellines, who no longer posed a threat as a political force.
8. On writing this, it occurs to me that Dante would certainly lack the "lyric" required by some modern editors.

judgement day when they will be sealed for eternity. Farinata rises dramatically out of a tomb. His back is straight and he looks contemptuously at all that surrounds him. He is obsessed with the political dimension and appears to be unconcerned about his own suffering; he is pained to hear of the fate of his Ghibelline faction. Cavalcante barely raises his head over the side of the tomb, and following a misunderstanding about who should know what, abruptly returns to his tomb weeping because he incorrectly believes that his son is dead. Cavalcante is myopic; Farinata is presbyopic. Farinata is the more fortunate, because in Dante's hell the damned can remember the past and perceive the future, but the present is unknown to them. Farinata explains:

> "We can see, like those in failing light,
> the things," he said, "that distant lie,
> only as much as the great Duke shines;[9]
> when they come close or are, entirely vain
> is our intellect; and if no one brings us news,
> we know nothing of your human state."[10]

We have here two characters, one comic and one tragic, who are inhabiting the same tomb and two different worlds. Cavalcante's world is the restricted one of his close family, from which he has been eternally separated by his heretical beliefs (Dante's

---

9. By 'great Duke' (*sommo duce*), Dante means 'God'. *Duce*, had been recently coined from the Latin *dux, ducis* (leader, military commander), which had also evolved over the centuries into two other Italian words: *doge* and *duca*. To add to the confusion, Dante uses the latter word to describe Virgil (*il mio duca*).
10. Dante Alighieri, *The Divine Comedy. Hell*, X, 100-105: "Noi veggiam, come quei c'ha mala luce,/ le cose", disse, "che ne son lontano;/ contanto ancor ne splende il sommo duce./ Quando s'appressano o son, tutto è vano/ il nostro intelletto; e s'altri non ci apporta,/ nulla sapem di vostro stato umano." Translation by the author.

judgements are brutally orthodox, but this does not interfere with the poetry). Farinata, the "magnanimous one" as Dante defines him, has a world that extends to the end of his vision, which goes into the future and into the past. Sadly that vision is becoming harder because God is turning off the lights, and after judgement day he will be sealed into eternal darkness. This only enhances his magnanimity and grandeur. He is free from remorse or concern for his own fate and still thinks like a statesman, as though he had just walked out of the *Palazzo della Signoria*, the Florentine seat of government.

* * * * *

The case of Dante presents the importance of balance, because both myopia and presbyopia have their weaknesses, which can only be overcome by the best of writers. For the myopic, anger is the greatest danger (I am sure there are great myopic rants, but they must be few and far between, and none are known to me). The reason is that myopic anger stinks like an unwashed body of animal force, and secretes the personal in its most petty and miserable state. Myopic writers are advised to keep it at bay and dance with wit and self-denigration to catch the absurd in the self and in us all, so the reader laughs in recognition of his own human flaws, relieved that he is not alone in harbouring them. Anger of course is a suitable subject for presbyopic literature. Some of the great works of literature are presbyopic rants.

Moralizing is the great danger for presbyopia. The writer risks putting himself at such a distance from his subjects that he feels above them. There never was much room for moral superiority in literature; now there is none. If presbyopic writing is to make a comeback, then it must learn humility and set itself modest tasks. Today presbyopic writers must limit themselves to going in search of small truths: the days of grandeur and the moralizing omniscient narrator are over, principally because there is no commonly held and clearly defined morality to work as a template for writer and reader.

The best writing is often a mix, and in the context of this essay the greatest writing is perhaps writing with normal vision: a clever and complex mix of the myopic and the presbyopic. But literary fashion pulls writers in different directions, and minor writers (without whom the greater writers could not exist) can play with extremes and redress the balance of literature when they go against the current. The time has come for some of us to be wilfully presbyopic, even if this occasionally means violating some fundamental laws of aesthetics.

Myopia examines passions up close and presbyopia does the same from a distance. The myopic writer has to live, while the presbyopic writer has to read and reflect. There is a delightful paradox here, a reversal in our imagery: presbyopic poets examine the far-off by locking themselves up in their studies with their books and their imaginations, whereas myopic poets need to seek inspiration by getting out into the world and producing experiences that they can write about. Myopia is governed by emotion and passion, while presbyopia is governed by reason. But this does not mean that myopic writers are more passionate and presbyopic ones more rational: good writing benefits from the tension between the author's character and the style and genre he chooses.

The presbyopic is often incapable of going beyond the posing of conflicting arguments without showing a preference for one in particular, whereas the myopic often, although not always, has a youthful certainty about it. The myopic gets things done and belongs to young cultures, whereas the presbyopic slows things and belongs to old ones. A friend laughingly asked me from the height of his full ninety years of life whether my theory of presbyopia meant that I was feeling old, and yet I have to say that the metaphor holds for ageing too. The young are more interested in answering questions and the old, as their vision fails them, become more interested in asking them. The young have inevitably read less and are more passionate and keen to experience life. They might have normal vision, but they are unlikely to suffer from presbyopia. In this collection, the Italian poems were mainly written during the eighties and, although not myopic, they are certainly less presbyopic. Italy had just undergone one of its sudden changes, and shifted from a highly politicised society to one that verged on apathy. When there was a slight spark of protest in the schools in the mid-eighties, I remember some teenagers returning home after school, and their parents, *sessantottini* both, solicitously asking whether they had been to the demonstration, as one might ask children whether they had done their homework. The teenagers unenthusiastically said that they had and shuffled down the corridor to throw their bags in their rooms. For me, the eighties meant a return to literature, and on rereading the Italian poems after so many years, I was struck by how many of them were concerned with a kind of guilt in indulging in so personal an activity, when the great issues remained unresolved. That concern now appears slightly odd. Firstly political passions are always short-lived for most people, and secondly the stories we tell each other have a powerful influence on our behaviour. Literature is not irrelevant, although sadly in the West, poetry might be.[11]

---

11. This is not universal: in Arab countries, for instance, poetry's influence remains incredibly strong.

After two centuries in which Romanticism has left its indelible mark on so much literature, at least in the sense of Romanticism as the "self-as-subject", and after one century of Freudian psychoanalysis, can we not tentatively suggest that self-obsession is also self-destructive? The natural obsessiveness of our psyche can be destructive for others as it can manifest itself in the form of political or religious fanaticism, but if channelled in the right direction, it can become the source of our creativity. I do not mean just our literary and artistic creativity, but for our present purposes, we will consider it in this restricted sense. "What is the point of poetry?" we hear people say. And the question is both fundamental and irritatingly banal. Poetry engages the obsessiveness of readers and writers. In the West, their numbers might be very limited, and poetry is no longer a very respected art, even though many who do not appreciate it would still not like to admit it publicly or in certain company (those of us who do enjoy poetry would probably prefer the honesty of those who openly admit their lack of interest). Neglect brings its own rewards, and I think that on the quiet quite a lot is being done. Poetry has fallen so low that we should not have overly ambitious plans for its renewal, but nor should we be defeatist. Besides it has suffered for over a hundred years from erudite elitists and demotic popularizers alike.

Why then write a literary manifesto when what stirrings there are – and there are some interesting ones – are pleasantly heterogeneous and unguided in a depressingly homogeneous and conformist world. Poetry finds its own channels organically, precisely because it is the most natural form of writing, which in turn is the most natural and least artistic of the arts. Like music, poetry's naturalness sometimes surprises because it is also a lover of form and thrives on the limitations imposed on it by tradition, language and cultural values. I know that I would cause offence if I were to say that "free verse" is a contradiction in terms. I admit that I am a little persuaded of this view, but am open to argument. One thing I think is clear: there is a necessary cycle whereby poets need to break the rules and run riot (what Nietzsche defined as the Dionysian) and then later poets have to rediscover and redeploy the methods and skills now thrown to one side (the Apollonian for Nietzsche). If, however, the Dionysian phase of the cycle leads to a complete rejection of all the rules, then the danger is that it will destroy not only the cycle, but poetry itself.

Overuse of and over-familiarity with form leads to mannerism. And then the cycle turns. Form becomes an impediment to art rather than its necessary equipment. Form needs to be reborn, but it must do so differently and find new ways to settle in with the ideas of a new generation. I have suggested that the distinction between myopia and presbyopia is related somewhat loosely to the distinctions between romanticism and classicism, and between the Dionysian and the Apollonian. Of these three distinctions which are themselves distinct, the one that most concerns form is the one between romanticism and classicism. However, the presbyopic must avoid the errors of post-modern architecture which can end up as a senseless bringing together of random, disconnected and shallow references to the classical;[12] the classical, which does not necessarily refer directly to antiquity because it may refer to a much later or even quite recent reincarnation of a classical form, is only damaged by being deified. It

---

12. On this point, I have been influenced by Salvatore Settis, whose contempt for post-modern *citazionismo* ("quotationism") in architecture is well argued in *The Future of the "Classical"* (Cambridge: Polity Press, 2006).

needs to be kicked about – but intelligently and as part of a whole (a pastiche will not do, however clever).

None of these terms are precise, partly because they get caught up in the history and periodisation of literature and art. I have seen Italian textbooks that define Shakespeare as a Mannerist, which caused me a little offence. He was quite definitely a Renaissance figure, and we should not be confused by the fact that the English Renaissance arrived a hundred years late – or actually rather early in the Northern European context, well-beaten only by the Dutch one. A cyclical analysis, like my own, does not infer that each cycle is identical – and we should never forget two important points: the cycles in different European countries are always out of sync and besides all good art is never purely anything. It is itself.

I wish to stress once again that I am not saying that the myopic viewpoint necessarily produces bad literature, and the great rebellion against the presbyopic was timely when it occurred two hundred years ago. Literature must constantly change course, as it burns out all the possibilities presented by a certain trend. Perhaps the time has come for another change in the artistic mood, and I do not think I am now entirely alone in being tired of the endless unburdening of often quite trivial personal sorrows and in-jokes, particularly as we are now in a world that is increasingly ill-at-ease with itself, tortured by immense ills in the present and menaced by cataclysmic predictions for the future. The artist does not always have to start from the "I". And those of us who don't, no longer have to be so much on the defensive.

I am concluding this introductory essay by examining some examples of myopia and presbyopia in contemporary poetry. I did consider the possibility of analysing an example of myopic writing at its most crass and self-obsessed, and I found a suitably extreme example. However I rejected the idea on the grounds that for me attacking individuals is only honourable if they are bigoted or if they are powerful, because the bigoted not only deserve to be paid in their own coin, they need to be, and the powerful represent more than themselves and have intentionally put themselves in that position.

I start then with Tom Pow's poem "St. Andrews", a poem that I like a great deal for several reasons, some of them personal. The poet in a rain-soaked Tuscan town reflects upon St. Andrews.

> I am sitting in Pitigliano –
> that human dovecot, perched
>
> on a spur of Tuscan rock –
> thinking about St. Andrews.

The perspective adopted by the poet is firmly that of his self. It places him in a foreign town unknown to him and to the reader, and relates both himself and this town to another town, one that is very familiar to the poet. These are "home thoughts from abroad". When I read these lines, I actually see the poet, a friend, languidly stretching his long body and his long vowels across a sofa in a flat darkened by the uncharacteristically ferocious and unremitting rain clouds of a Tuscan February, and gently cursing his luck. The average reader has not stood in that particular viewpoint, and the question is whether the poet manages to bring the reader into that viewpoint and justify the wide-angle perspective. I believe he does, but my privileged proximity to the viewpoint makes it difficult for me to know with certainty. The poem continues with increasing lightness:

> It's not so hard. February
> in Tuscany's not how the pictures

> play in your mind. I've seen
> the charm of small-town piazzas
>
> drabbed by a relentless
> East coast rain and otherwise
>
> delightful alleys so grey and cold
> you'd think them splashed with salt.
>
> But, this evening, the day turned
> and, from the valley of the Meleta,
>
> Pitigliano appeared to float
> on its honeyed rock against
>
> a properly azure sky.
> In memory, once again, I saw
>
> how St. Andrews would likewise
> stoke up all the clarity
>
> an East coast day could offer,
> till the town, miraculously, rose
>
> on a bed of its very own golden
> Tuscan light. At such times,
>
> from within the warmth
> of its evening walls, I'd hear
>
> ringing out soundlessly –
> over cornfields, turnip drills and sea –
>
> the ghostly finger
> of its ruined campanile.[13]

The poem does what myopic poetry should do: it invites the reader into the poet's viewpoint in such an attractive manner that the reader does so willingly. It engages in description, a description of the nature and architecture that surrounds the poet's being and creates his mood. It reflects that mood in the slow and light rhythm of the poetry. But the poet has to do more

---

13. Tom Pow, *In the Becoming* (Edinburgh: Birlinn, 2009), p. 231.

than that, and Pow achieves this by a comparison with St. Andrew's. This creates a tension in the viewpoint, and you sense, although the poet never tells you, that he has had a more permanent relationship with the East Coast town. I happen to know as a privileged reader that St. Andrew's was Pow's university. However, the poem is accessible because, apart from the delicious lightness of its sounds, it establishes in few words some very interesting themes concerning places and the sense of comfort (or lack of it) felt within them. The poem emphasises the similarities between home and abroad, and how they both partake of the bleak and the bright. He also suggests, nicely, that home over time partakes more of the bleak, and this other place more of the bright. A cosmopolitan ease pervades the poem and is its most attractive quality.

Sandie Craigie's myopic poem, "Mirror", appears to examine the myopic:

> And I ... care not for vanity
> nor idle conversation
> around the word – ME
>
> And you ... in all your depths
> can but reflect
>
> Yet I have fallen for
> your clear persuasions
> that what you show
> is all there is to see
>
> And you ... through time
> have drowned the child in me
>
> Yet somewhere in your eyes
> I saw a young girl
> but time has stolen,
> I have grown old
>
> How foolish now.
> I came to you, believing

> Oh Mirror, you,
> I thought you knew my soul.[14]

The success of a myopic poem like this is that its viewpoint has a certain universality. The poem says little about the writer and a great deal about what it is to be a human being (or at least one who owns a mirror). The mirror as a metaphor for looking out of oneself and into oneself is a powerful one. The simplicity of the language requires a good poet.

Next I would like to examine briefly a couple of presbyopic poems, the first by a very fine poet, Eleanor Brown. It is "The Oak Room":

> Three hogs, stuffed into three expensive suits;
> of one dead branch, three bloated, stinking fruits;
> three scabrous chunks of English Upper Crust,
> one avarice, one gluttony, one lust;
> slurred words brayed out between their flagging jaws,
> drink-laden lost consonants and ravaged vowels;
> three hairlines, horror-stricken, flee away
> from sweating brows and bloodshot eyes; pink-grey,
> indulged and sagging excess flesh aquiver –
> O grant them soon cirrhosis of the liver,
> our English God. Whom, on our English knees,
> we thank for public schools, and men like these.[15]

I chose this example partly because I admire this poet and partly because of its clear similarities with my own poem in this collection: the bilingual untitled poem on page 26. Hers is a better and more presbyopic poem (mine, which has a very small element of first-person narration, was originally written in another country and is less witty). Interestingly, she has made her examples of middle-class smugness male, and I made

---

14. *The Big Green Yonkly*, ed. by Billy Cornwall and Mike Dillon (Edinburgh: Rookbook, 1992), p. 61.
15. Eleanor Brown, *Maiden Speech* (Tarset: Bloodaxe Books, 1996), p. 18.

mine female. My poem is one of only four that are based on real events (the others being "Jan Paweł" – p. 7, "Reflections on being told that Gaels ..." – p. 33, and "Fascism Encountered in a City Park" – p. 41), and I believe that Brown's former public-schoolboys also existed. I was practically run down by two fur-coated, middle-class, well-fed women under the *portici* of Pisa's Borgo Stretto, whereas she may well have had some dismal encounter in an English pub. Bad manners are not restricted to the middle classes, but they are aggravated by the smugness sometimes associated with that burgeoning section of our society. Perhaps the presbyopic poet is only inspired to write about real experience when it is in some way distasteful. Satirists – those spiteful and entirely necessary gadflies – are as presbyopic as they are dyspeptic.

The next poem is by the quintessential presbyopic poet, whose righteous anger is drummed out with a fascinating rhythm of sounds and ideas. To listen to Tom Leonard's poetry is to listen to a fiery prophet of humanism, who never lets you forget that the world's absurdities also include brutal and pointless injustices. Readers who go on to look at my own poetry will immediately note that while Leonard and I differ considerably in our poetic style, we often share a great deal in our poetic intent:

> state killing is not killing
> state killing is justifiable context
> state killing is the operation of justice
>
> stateless killing is simply killing
> stateless killing is never context
> stateless killing is motiveless evil
>
> we are the state of oppression
> is genocide
>
> to accuse the state of racism
> is genocide

> to accuse the state of colonial expansion
> is genocide
>
> no one wants to be accused of genocide
> much better turn a blind eye

In this extract from his long poem, "The Proxy Badge of Victimhood",[16] Leonard uses the anaphora repeatedly. This rhetorical device involves the repetition of the initial words of a line, generally over three lines. Here it is used obsessively not only for its poetic effect, but also to underscore what I call the aesthetics of ideas. Ideas or assertions are counterposed, but the reader is clear as to which have integrity and which do not.

I have never suggested that I have initiated presbyopic poetry or a return to it. Tom Leonard has been around for a long time, and more recently there have been many more examples. Its time has very probably come, and its fate certainly does not hang on this collection of poetry with its many failings – both those of which I am aware and those of which I am not. The primary purpose of this essay is not to introduce my own poetry but to make a statement on where poetry might go, particularly if it is to regain some of its lost significance in Western society.

* * * * *

I started this essay with a quote from De André's song "The Optician", which also uses sight and its distortions as a metaphor for the ways in which we interpret this world:

> *The colour-blind, the presbytes and those who beg for sight!*
> *The trader in light, your optician,*
> *has fickle set his sights solely on uncommon customers*
> *who little care for normal vision.*

---

16. Tom Leonard, *Being a Human Being* (Glasgow: Object Permanence, 2006).

An optician no longer, he trafficks in lenses
for improvising eyes of contentment,
so that pupils in the habit of copying
start to invent the worlds they have to observe.
 (Fabrizio de André, "The Optician", my translation)

This metaphor of sight is a very common one – a dead metaphor as in our usage of the verb "to see" as a synonym for "to understand", but in the hands of the skilled songwriter it can be brought back to life. De André is himself an excellent example of a presbyopic writer, and an expert in the narrative song. He satirises the rich and powerful, and extols the virtues of prostitutes, hopeless lovers and the clinically depressed. He mitigates his criticisms of an anarchist bomber by comparing his violence with that of warmongering politicians (and today this pacifist songwriter would undoubtedly fall foul of legislation banning the "glorification of terrorism"). Anyone who knows his songs, must also know his atheistic Christian morality, his perceptive irony and his deep love for suffering humanity, expressed with such poignant irony throughout his work. The Algerian immigrant workers with whom I shared a spartan dormitory above an only slightly more comfortable *pensione* in Florence in the early seventies were enormous fans of De André's music, and I fancy that De André would have been greatly heartened to have amongst his most devoted admirers these intelligent polyglot young men destined to a life of monotonous jobs in a system designed to keep them on the margins of society. Undoubtedly there will be several biographies on this eccentric singer and songwriter who briefly caught the imagination of a generation and a culture, but I am not inclined to seek them out. We need know no more about De André, because in these times of talentless celebrities he was that most wonderful of things: a creative nobody.

Presbyopia

Presbyopia

(for this collection)

My sight it fades
and fading faded forms reveals;
ageing looks beyond its age
to shrivelled centuries beyond decades.

My understanding shrinks
but by shrinking, shrunken heroes highlight
the grandeur of the passing age
and heap high the majesty of many
whose uniform uniqueness struts the stage.

Our history speeds
and speeding slows the pulse
of time. And all the ages,
all the peoples of this peopled world
are one, and one they are
within this weeping world of wars
unequal to the task of resolving
their unequal sides.

And as the image fades,
some fading truth that can be grasped
flickers from the dismal shades.

Auto-da-fé (or How I burnt a planet at the stake)

Will you forgive me now, you hurted shadows of my future self?
I walk and breathe the salted air as pure as when my fathers'
                                                      fathers walked
and left a world untainted by their use of it. Not I.
Not I, the pampered, sophisticated seigneur of our technologic age,
that mindless burns the antiquated substance of the earth itself.
We have no use of it beyond its usage now. That is our stated
                                                              claim.

Your skins are sores, as sores will suppurate upon polluted earth.
Your hair it falls like clumps of hay to mock the balded barren land
that cries out thirsted beneath the greenhouse of the sky.
Your lips they curse your cursed fathers of a special age
which left unpaid the debt each generation pays and indebted you
for follies that were theirs alone.

I stand and conquer all before, as I am granted by my right to life,
my right to this and right to that, and leave unrighted all the poor,
and all the many blighted generations that are to come
like blinded soldiers of that Great War who led each other hand in
                                                              hand
and broken head to withered shoulder across the blasted land,
discarded by my greed, and onwards to a place unknown – to an
                                                         earth unmanned.

Rebirth of the gods

The gods they went in ancient times
into their shallow graves – and godlike never died,
but slept and dreamt and cried.
The loose earth shuddered, no grass could grow,
no beast could burrow, no water flow.
And all who passed could feel the warmth,
the trembling life, the broken will, the wish
to rise up once again and fill our hearts
with chaos.

For many years these quivering graves
were held in check by a god who saves
all those who call him by his proper name
and mutter form and charge the air
with a syntax of their choosing.
And God who flies in the higher sphere
was lost from view, no longer clear
through words that swarm and keep all hearts
in irons.

Then came a man who opened graves,
embraced these underfed seraphic slaves
and bid them go analyse the psyche,
become new gods to paralyse the psyche.

But how they'd changed
since when they fled Olympus and its city,
and lay within the dampened earth
and bled beneath the barren mulch that kept them from
                                                      man's pity.
Their sunken chests, their hacking coughs, their staring
                                                       eyes
that couldn't see, but stared again upon the godlike mortals.
They saw them run within machines, and conjure up their
                                                  image of
a godlike feast to play with. "What shall we do?" the gods
they cried, "What can we do with men who are made of
                                                     mettle?"
The man who toyed with Psyche simply said, "Take control!
And hold them, kindless kill their will and captivate their
                                                  mental means
to think and reason."

But how they'd changed since when they fled,
and soon forgot their lovely names; misled
they were by the man who plays with Psyche,
their leader now by the last act of winged Tyche.*

What were these names he chose to place upon
resurrect Olympians? First came Id who could perform
no unruly instinct worthy of his nature.

He shuffled by, and then came youthful Ego, her form
so frail, and half asleep. "No, no, dear Will, you cannot
                                                    choose;
I must consult the conscious, or was it *the* unconscious
                                                    self?
This job's so hard, and harder still to answer why we're here
to play these parts within the parts of mettled people."

Then came Superego, what a sight! This twisted *bodach*[†]
trimmed his beard and finger-pointed here and there,
and there and here, and endless called the acts of others
into question. He stood and glared upon the crowd
of mettled men, and they slowly mangled him and all his
                                                    heap
of prohibitions.[‡]

---

[*] Tyche: the Greek god of fortune.
[†] *Bodach*: the Gaelic for "old man".
[‡] This poem was suggested in part by Borges's short story *Ragnarök*, whose gods were "testaments to the degeneration of the Olympian line" and were summarily shot by outraged human beings.

The loser

Have you seen him shuffle by? His whitened flesh and sickly eye?
He brought it on himself. Old man he is, and old before his time;
for who could credit what he did? He did so little but what he did
was stubborn foolish, a folly fixed upon a whim, a childish thing.
He said all men are equal, when it was still the modish way
to play with all these grand ideas that no one really holds for true
within their soul, within the inner order of their ordered minds.
He did, and then continued to believe when all around had meekly
admitted to the error of their ways, and their fond youth
was little more than youthful go and get up to another place,
more comfortable to our increasing needs. And yet he fell apart,
and headstrong held to that one truth, while falling and parting
for his way, his lonely way of wanting justice for the damned.

Jan Paweł

(On seeing a statue of John Paul II
outside a church in Elbląg)

What does a man have to do
to have statues made of him?
Of simple, sketched and lifeless likeness
of himself? Of engrandised self
launched off on non-mortality that lasts
but one regime or two? And then is curio.

And curious, too, that you, a man of God,
sought out the company of Panowie Lenin
and Franz Joseph set in bronze
and stone, like so many manikins
who, posing, pose no threat
and prance immobile in these structured
structures of our brains, on which
the powerful rely.

*Lines scribbled on hearing on the radio that a clever "neuro-economist" has proven that GDP always makes us happy**

How could I believe now that spring is gone
and all the world brought stutteringly low
shuttered in the closedness of its darkened self?
The rotting sinews of my living corpse continue
to propel me on my onward track to stunted thoughts
that blossom like a winter bud half blasted
by its reckless act of doing things out of its time.
I see no sudden movements on the hill that meets the sky,
and hear no daring discourse that harries swelling ranks
of fierce and ruthless folk, or follows hard upon some truth
that hits like a lightning bolt and carries me aloft – away
from me and all the humdrum of the hopeless contrivance
of my living in this over-measured, mechanistic consortium
of hopeless human consumership all stacked upon the shelves
that hold no hopes beyond themselves.

And all is truly gone, and has no size within its distant shape –
a past is shrunken and who recalls the real kindness of an act
that sprang from beliefs beyond the moneyed motions
of our selfish gene?

---

* The great Gaelic poet, songwriter and political activist, Murdo MarPharlane, considered it a great compliment to say of a friend that he could survive for a month on one block of tobacco. He had a better measure of what success and happiness are.

Have I not finished yet?

Have I not finished with calling comrades to their arms
to go forth and fight, and fight once more
for that great certitude, that war to end all wars,
that shining city of delights where all are free.
Have I not finished yet?

Have I not finished with calling to my God's grey beard
to curse and kill the other men who toil in ignorance
and do not share my chosen certitudes that lift me up,
console my soul and make me more than any other man.
Have I not finished yet?

Have I not finished with calling for my servant's tray
to bring me all that's good and sweet without a thought
for those outwith my kingdom of consumer wealth,
for lesser men who should have less than I.
Have I not finished yet?

Of course I have not finished yet. I am a man,
and a man is all these things and none
and more besides, and can be never done
with learning to unlearn what he should not forget.
Of course I have not finished yet.

Utilitarianism

This word, it has no feel,
no texture to its call
upon our greed,
upon the selfish inner self,
the barren core they say we are,
and are indeed but more besides.
What use are we if uselessly
we merely want and take, ingest,
expel the substance of substantial waste?

What is the need this withering age
of greed demands, but nothing can assuage?
What heart, what soul, what cause, what goal
could speed the pulse and stir the senses quicker?
It is upon an aimless sky that clouds perform
their passive motion. It is upon a passive people
financial forces force them aimless on
to petty things that sparkle.

Elegy for Orwell

Not since he saw the purple shoots of heaven
pictured in his mind – all visions of collective acts
shining through the English lands, had he
encountered such a heightened sense
of what it is to be.

Then he wrote and does so now, unflagging
in his wish to see a better division of our lots, a chance,
frustrated thing that lives but in a moment of its onward flight
to hope, the created matter of our thoughts, our little minds
which hold infinities within the skewered notions, greasy chains
of neurons that have no rest – a substance that always disappoints
and leaves us looking for the next big thing that leads us on.
It is delightful gambol and a jig, if everyone could dance,
but who would gyrate and disco, rock or techno on the floor,
if all the others carry chains to slow the movements of their brains
and feet. He'd rather not.

The academician disburses help to those who write
within the strictures plutocrats impose upon us all,
who do not share our writer's rectitude. What does he do
for our scribbler in a threadbare suit unravelling
as he ravels words to lead us through confusing tangles
of what could and should and would be done, if only
we were free of insane ladders of desire constructed

by those abject priests who perceive us as a mechanic thing
that clockwork ticks away its time upon this world
in obsessed pursuit of self and all the little trinkets
they produce? The academician snorts and cries,
"A better tone I would expect from educated man
who holds his pen correctly in his hand and rightly
considers how each tiny coin perfectly balanced
in the flow of trade will reward each labour and reflect
true value of every little act or thing. If there is intrigue,
then it is just that people starve to fatten up its fruits.
If there is folly, innocence and love, then who can stop
the cunning from making fools of fools, and cutting low
the crop of riches that feed the grandeur of deserving folk."

Our man? He scorns this all, rejects their pride and proudly
carries on his solitary path, upsetting them and setting
off the human hounds well-trained in keeping tabs
on independent thought. These sorry fools are always found
in any corner of the globe, but on occasions overbreed,
run riot, and become the purpose of the state, be it
right or left. Later he would speak to these, his one mistake,
the blemish on his great career.

He went to Spain, fought hard to stop the phalanx hate
had built within a nation's privileged elite, and took a bullet
to the neck, and spurted blood along a line that could not hold
against the power of the powers that ruled Europe and held

in place the measured dreams of myriads of myriads
who always felt that life had left them uninvited to the feast.

And still he wrote, his vision cracked,
his hopes dispersed like routed soldiers
taken by surprise and hounded
till their feet were heavy with the dirt
which clayey sticks and drags down the soul
to pits where pity loses all its aura
of human will and hope to share our common course.

And so he wrote his confusing complex message
to us all; not a call to arms –
a call to thought that structures well
our needs for freedom, equal rights and peace,
and holds aloft his shattered dream
beautied by its fracture and steeped
in all the many sorrows of our great cause.

We should hope that the social ism
shall have its day, but will not last,
for nothing does; remember that.
Avoid the cult of believing far too much,
of making hopes a hard-sealed truth
that gives ferocious finger-waggers power to play
with their sadistic certitudes: the eternal boot
that crushes human face.

The Emperor Hack

They clapped you to your throne room,
they clapped you through the hall
of gleaming screens of numbers
that measure – size the treasure
you built upon the word.

In the beginning it was heard
how from your modest childhood,
little more than a newspaper
to cover your back, and a local one at that,
you came to cover continents and were crowned the emperor hack.

You came to cover continents with floods of words to back
the helpless rich whose champion we sadly seemed to lack.
You took your words and poured them by the tonload in your
                                                      trucks,
and though the words were weary they returned in the form of
                                                      bucks.
You stood upon the poopdeck as you took your flagship home,
The Sun it set on a foaming sea and left the venturers to roam.
News of the World came to your ears of wars and pending doom,
but you published then a picture of tits in mellow bloom.
Our people they were sickened by the square box in the room,
so you doubled up the channels and you held them in the gloom
of doubtful jollities and ciphers whom you groom
to be the very thing they're not and not to be the thing they are,
the very obverse of a star they call a human being.

Enough of silliness and rhyme, I have a question
and it pertains to time, the thing that helps us on our way,
to wrinkles, sores and slow decay.
I have a question and it is this:
what makes a man like you press on
to pressure us and repress us too
with a press that has no heart to feel,
nor truth to tell of earthly hell?
It is to this dark tissue of our lives
that you should turn, and not to the heavy substance
of your stock. Or else it will weigh with the weight of years
that take you to the dying bed the rich await with fears,
the poor with glee to free their weightless souls.

You complain, summon rulers from distant lands
to pay you court; for they want words warmed up for them.
And you concede, but first you make them plead.
You let them plead, so they will know who has the power
to empower. Until they hear the rattle.
Then will their words, their shameless words, come out to battle.
Your last croaking word will be the signal for a war of words
that'll bury, scorn, unthrone you in its prattle.

Empire

There is no love nor special thing that can survive
the teeming, darkened corridors of want.
And what is true is true no more,
when hammered by propaganda's empty words of,
"We thank thee Lord for having made us free
to rule the world and liberate its inner need to be
so much more like us."

Progress

So little it came to me the thought
of what we could have done. So slight
the dream of things to come, I wore
it lightly on my back; I swore its coming
was like the coming of the spring,
a thing so natured by its seasoned source
it had no choice but to follow fated course.

And now. The heavy autumn winds come in
to shriek and din the empty-headed dolefulness
that duly asks, "What is it now we have we did not have
before we came, and came so certain of the fullness
of our times?" "The shrunken grape, our passite past,*
it has no wrath, no hope to go to passions fast
upon the passioned anger at killing fields still here
to weigh our wings with catastrophes and fear.

The city high within our minds is full of cheer.
And in it walk the shadows of our better selves.
The whitened walls and heightened arts swell full –
the pull of all the shining spires of hope, the fires
of reason and towers of altruistic rectitude.
Not crude but complex paradigms of pleasure
can still live here within the fearless fantasy
that treasures human and not inhuman fortitude.

---

* passite: invented from the Italian *passito* for over-ripe grapes that
have started to pucker on the vines under the autumn sun.

State-indoctrinated doggerel

(written shortly after the miners' strike – a distant time)

We're in a state, a real state,
the state the state has put us in.
It's put us in a state of fear
of boundaries and words and race.
It's put us in a state of grace,
feeling better than any other place.
It's put us in a state of nerves
– serve the country and whom it serves.
Serve it well and come up strong.
You'll never know what's right and wrong.
Troublemakers want just to be seen,
they never work and are rarely clean.
What's this! It took away my job,
and treated me like some lefty slob.
It had me hit with a heavy stick,
and had me judged by some pompous prick.
Good citizens don't deserve this fate;
my world is crushed – in a sorry state.
Oh what a state the state is in.

The second telling

That war with wings of death does twist and crush and kill
the flimsy leathered bag of flesh and bone and liquid life
that spills upon the sands,
requires no second telling.

That might with wings borne up upon the deathless lust
for power, does twist and crush and kill the fragile fabric
of the truth that surges in the molten matter of the mind,
requires no second telling.

That brains are battered with a hundred myths and calls
to join the crowd that crowds within its little understanding
of the battered brains and flesh that melt into the mud,
requires no second telling.

That heat and fumes and fire scorch the fleeting moments
of the momentary news machines that leave their litter
in our thoughts like plastic wrappers on the desert floor,
requires no second telling.

That lives are cheap and cheaper still the lives of those
who have no voice within the corridors of confidence,
where smiling lips of certainty breath the air-cooled comfort
of knowing they are right,
requires no second telling.

Tell it not. Who does not know Fallujah burns?
The rains will come, and wash away the rotted matter
of war with rivulets of cant which cannot quite
remove from sight the shadows of what was and is no more.

Captain R and the culture of impunity

"I do my job," the big man said,
"Embody demos cracy's fairest ways,
uphold it through its civilising phase
of fire and sword and shock and awe.
To make them suffer; that's our plan,
is what we bravely fight on for."

Frightened Iman lost her way and took
a burning bullet to the leg and fell.
You have no demos, little girl,
no nation, rights, no voice to tell
of how you've suffered at the gates of hell.

Up spoke bold Captain R and drew his big man body up,
and swung his blackened rifle round to kill,
"She moved defenceless to the east," his colleague called,
"she's just a girl.' "Of cockroach stock," the big man starts to
                                                                          still
his rifle to her head and fires the force that strikes her dead.
He turns, his job well done and marches proudly to the west,
but then he turns again, so wedded is he to his job,
a stickler, thorough to the last, he blasts away his big black gun,
delights the playground of his little mind, and burning lead
mangles bones and pretty face. He is the best,
a big man by whom we are impressed.

Little Iman, I only know your death and from afar
I grieve and comprehend no longer how such silence
falls on silent death and how we turn and look not back.
You did your job, you little man, you Captain R,
you killed the girl and lifted up your cruel star
of hate.

But tell me now what is your job, your sacred violence?
Where will it lead? What does it say of you and yours?
Is that a man, big or small, who does these things?
You love to hate, and killing cause less willing folk
to hate as well. Such is your job.

Iman al-Hams was murdered in cold blood by Captain R, who approached the thirteen-year-old girl lost on her way to school and possibly attempting to avoid other danger points. She had already been wounded in the leg by an Israeli soldier and could not move. After having killed her with two bullets to the head, he turned back and emptied his gun into her, and doctors found seventeen bullets in her body. It may have been this last act of gratuitous violence against a dead body that prompted somebody to hand over recordings of the radio conversations. The Israeli army originally claimed that the girl was thought to have been a suicide bomber and a frightened soldier shot her. We are therefore supposed to feel sorry for the poor soldier and angry at the perfidious nature of his enemy. In fact the terrified girl was at least 100 yards away from any soldier, and according to the chatter on the army radios, "a little girl", "scared to death" and "running defensively eastward". Captain R was of the opinion that "anything moving in the zone, even a three-year-old, needs to be killed". This command was in breach of the Geneva Convention. Even an enemy fighter, let alone a terrified and entirely innocent girl, should be taken prisoner and given medical assistance, if wounded and unarmed. Lieutenant-General Rafael Eitan, who planned the attack on Lebanon with Sharon, referred to Palestinians as "drugged cockroaches scurrying in a bottle", and suggested that "We have to do everything to make them so miserable that they will leave." Unfortunately for stateless thirteen-year-old Iman al-Hams, that possibility was not open to her. Following the release of the tapes, the Israeli authorities charged Captain R, but unsurprisingly he was acquitted in spite of the overwhelming evidence. On the day of his acquittal, a well-informed and, for such a subject, unusually forthright journalist on the *Today* programme tackled an Israeli spokesman. Angered that she had examined the details of the case, he simply shouted that everyone knows that Israel has one of the best legal systems in the world.

The same day that Iman died, another girl was shot through the head by a sniper's bullet as she stooped to put something in the oven. Her brains exploded over the mother who had kept her home because she thought that would be the safest place.

Captain R received compensation amounting to about $17,000 for wrongful prosecution. For this one act, the Israeli judicial system reveals itself as no more than a cruel farce. At least Captain R's military colleagues were sufficiently revolted by his behaviour to report him to an army radio station – significantly choosing to ignore the proper authorities – and when soldiers who are trained to kill show better judgement than those who should be trained solely to express ponderous and detached rulings, a state has become crippled by its own inability to understand its future. Justice – requiring the child murderer behind bars and compensation paid not to him but to Iman's family – will not resolve the conflict, but it would wipe from the slate possibly the worst case of two measures that are differentiated on the basis of "race" and religion And we all – poets, novelists, artists, journalists and politicians who love to express our various opinions – cannot pass by on the other side and leave outrage to some future generation. To do so would be to scratch our souls on the jagged edges of prejudice. Silence is not an option. My poem is an attempt to calm the revulsion that invades me every time I think of this terrible incident.

Un eroe del nostro tempo
(The poem on the next page is a loose
English translation of this one)

Vorrei esser nato
rampollo d'uno stato
di canonica durezza
che mi tenesse a cavezza;
allora sì, con fiel in bocca
mi sfogherei la rabbia
contro grettezza che s'arrocca
nel castello sulla sabbia;
ribalterei la norma
la forma rinnoverei,
entusiasta sull'orma
d'eroica virtù. Sosterrei
l'insostenibile.

A hero of our time

(or A young man discovers ideals, authority,
powerlessness and a desire for power)

To be the offspring of a taut-strung state
the rigid regiment of thought, and fate
held in its distant godhead nation,
invisible soul of petty machination,
is my desire.

For then could I well justify the fire
that burns when the wideness of the world
the child perceived is shrunken by the lanky limbs
of youth to whom the sullen meanness is unfurled
by reaching above the parapet of parental trust,
distance diminished by the distant view
of crowded commonplace,
discovered the joy of the joyless face.

For then could I give vent
to all the pent-up anger against the castle
constructed on the shifting sands,
tear at the wall with bleeding hands,
believe in better worlds, built and buttressed
by our solid dreams, by the martyred word
of truth upholding the absurd.

(The untitled poem that follows is then followed by an English translation)

Signore impellicciate, visi gravi,
vanno per il Borgo Stretto,
sguardi scolpiti nella cipria
solcano appena il mio pensiero.
Signore sostenute da saldi principi,
da mariti professionisti,
il mento vi sprofonda
nel cuscino grinzoso consunto
baciato dalla freddezza
dell'abitudine, vostra sicurezza.

      Grave glares on fur-enfolded shoulders,
      stare in the void of Oxford Circus,
      moulded in moistening cream and powders,
      they barely touch the movement of my mind,
      move solidly on solid principles,
      well-husbanded with the professional kind.
      Ladies, your chirling chins sag in waxing
                  waves of fat,
      kissed by lips chilled and habit entwined.

Matter that little matters...

I often well-evaded words will search
in searching to affirm myself,
the little man, whose longed-for line
would time en_case, and parcel up
those joys, that each the meagre twine
as yet uncut will allocate, and which
the sullen Parchae interlace
with coarser threads, those golden darts.
And then the cut;
the stuff is trussed and wound around;
atom-tight, the fading ball is placed upon the stack.
Who will consume and thus unthread this fast-decaying
                                                matter of the past,
and who will read the latent phonemes
punched within the solid moulds and cast
within the rigid rhythms of my mind.

I took the puzzle down ...

I took the puzzle down,
trainbound, in the car,
supine smoothly bedslung,
amongst the rushed flow
of human integers,
the indivisible cells of thought,
I turned it over,
felt its weight,
and duly pondered in the bath,
or corn-flakes crunching in that lucidity
of morning haze,
its full extent, its width, its length,
the inner puzzles, part results
and still...
it fled, it teased, it entertained
and cursed perhaps my arrogance
and cried: "Give up, accept the arms of ritual
and routine, embrace all those
who do not care about the race of time;
suck in the sordid juices of despair,
the ready-made realities for the ruled;
let the all-consuming daemon of consumption
quell the inner fires of your humanity,
inscribe dark foreboding letters on a thrombosed heart.

The North Sea

Deathly, the sucking sea
assails the slope of shifting sands
and drags me on.
Silent wanderer
it hugs the lands,
that great quantity of unknown sleep.

It waits watchingly and is watched.
How good it is to see
and not to touch
with screaming soul
the long, gull-grey, gull-bobbing swell.

Hope and the red hero

Spring eternal! Second sister and most human
of the three majuscule maidens,
high-sounding on priest pursed lips,
the trinity of virtue.
Fickle friend and demiurge of dreams,
you help us skyward build the themes
of our collective happiness,
and fill with greater substance
the cold steel coffins of reality.
How hollow sounds the hardness
of all that we can touch;
the folly of your ether will I barter for his coarse clutch
How unreal is your realism,
socialist soldier on the move.
My hand in hers I will follow for
I do prefer your youthful spirit,
your belief in us or what we could be,
and even your fanatic fight,
to the murder and the greed-gorged dismemberment
of our collective corpse,
hard-heralded by the vultures of the right.

Religion

To You the smoothing swarm of years,
close-shadowed by that finite end,
have turned my thoughts, my heart perhaps,
but not my faith.
Will that the sagging spring of life bring on?
To follow in the feet of fears
so natural to our unnatured state.
You softened the sorrow,
when I did fret within the frigid frame
of this "I", this "my", this "me" that restless turns
and paces the grey-celled cell that is my brain,
the reason for my reason that reason spurns.

Poets without passion

The frozen form of a past pensively wrought
from cold iron – the heavy hinges creak,
the gate slams shut. And yet
I still would stare upon that tomb of passions
chilled by the wind of change.

Fool! Nothing can be learnt in there.
The skeleton now lacks the flesh –
hopes whose feeble breath was lost
within the marble blast.

It is to warmth and sweet-lipped smiles,
and heady laughter hurled from heavy juices,
to the quickening pace of slower limbs,
and yes, to this drowning earth,
that I must turn the blurred and blunted
conceits of concentration.

A simple thought when neatly told
will defy mass, grow bigger than itself.
The sincere secluded in their truth
and the innocent cry out for words of weight.
We deaden what it is to feel
so we may make our feelings felt.

**Reflections on being told that Gaels are lazy
by an urbane Englishman on a beach in Tiree**

There is, it's said, a soul to that,
the managed man who cleanly cuts
his actions to the manner of his time,
and laughs.
A baroque well-suited hybrid of a modern man
who smiling greets me across a guarded fullness of himself,
he laughs:
The lazy Gaels who furnished him his empire on the heights,
and more besides who fell, and did not fall but vanished
in the clearing, cleaning ethnic war they fought in peace
that stopped our tongue with the Cheviot fleece.

The greater spirit thinks those greater that it meets,
but this man's spirit spurns and scoffs:
The lazy Gaels who cut and carried in the peats,
who drove the fattened cows to fatten foreign lords.
The Gaels whose houses burnt like burning weeds,
to plant the lands with fruitless Cheviot seeds.

The door is open or the door is shut,
the heart is feeling or the mind is sprung,
the skin is hardened or the soul is stung;
but this man's heart and mind are cut
and tailored to a standard form
that laughs:
The lazy Gaels that carved a culture from a sea and land
cut by grandness, harshness, divine and ancient force,
that holds hard to the centre of the things that count;
for those who listen let stories still be heard.
This soul-less soul while tramping on the tragic stage,
sees only sands surrounding some exotic bird.

Zarathustra's Last Interview

"Promise me this," he said.
"Stay not the onward movement of your mind
and hold your course when barren talk
pervades, and has no scope or sense
that drives and makes unconscious conscious thought"

He stood, and waving wide the circle of his hand,
he lifted up his spear. "The huddled dwellings on the hill
are not a home to change; and when the fighters
                      fall upon the plain,
the dullards shudder in their beds and weep their fears,
                      as though the gods could care
a damn about the frightened witless fools who fail to flee
the wrathful ruthless horde – the company of the strong."

"I have no quarrel with the settled folk," I said.
"Nor I," without a strain he stretched his arm
and pointed spear, its shining head, towards the tidy shacks,
"they are the mass, the herd, the herded demos whom we mock,
they built that fence to keep us out,
                      and considered it an act of will,"
he laughed , "but all they did was build a pen
                      and turn themselves to sheep.
For it is right that man should walk or ride
                      upon the mountain ridge,
and carry spear and thrust it deep to make himself a man indeed."

"Who fashioned you that glinting spike of death?"
      I asked and waited for the rift.
"A man whose skill is just our stock –
      to be culled and killed as we would wish,
and if we are wise, we always leave some living
      to keep extant that breed of forge-hands,
sowers of seed that flocks the plain,
      and all the other settled, soulless men."
The sinewed sage, vigoured by his years,
      drew in his breath and raised his spear
above his head, half threat – half gesture of his will to power.

"A force," I said, "whose only justification is its force,
      and has no pleasure
but its exercise cannot be good, and good is when
      the soul divests itself of power,
accepts its moral equalness." "Ha!" he cried,
      and joyous danced around the spear
he'd skewered to the ground, "the vapid niceness of this man!
      But what of life,
and nature too! Does the lion lick the lamb's wounds or bite?
And does it run or aimless sit and make a meal of a meal
      after having mealy-mouthed
mouthed a prayer to God? It has no god and nor should we."

"I heard the clamour of your words in little Europe's agora, and felt
the textured smoothness and the heavy lightness of their weave,
their troubled truths, alluring lies, and clever, clever talk. You do
speak true when speaking of the little things, but not the big:
who are the strong who, unlike you, must travel in a pack?

And like a flood, a plague, a horde of certitudes go cutting down
the lives of industry and industry itself. What do you gain?"

"What do they lose?" he laughed again, "if losing
                  lets them start once more
to build upon their knowledge of the things
                        this world contains. They scurry
with their social mind and their own minds are not their own.
              They worry,
as retainers of the rich, they slave for us,
                  the strong who know the reason
for which we came into this world: good war
                     which hallows any cause, and more
was made from its courageous course
                      than fretting with one's neighbour's fate.
The fools! They value love – that soporific state –
                    and underrate the force of hate."
"This is hubris; this is intellect that holds
                    high opinion of itself and structured ways
to be a man. It belongs to you but not to them, the company that flays
the folk who work and love and hope
                    in less engrandised circumstance,"
I answered him with bitter rectitude.
              "For you would condemn chance
to always favour bold and not reflective men
                  unless they think like you.
Your gayness is your rash redress for what your father never knew:
the power of pleasure and the pleasure of the power
                  to take what pleasure wants
and should not have."

Down they came, the company of power, and what a motley crew:
one wore a helmet, one a tricorn hat,
                          one dressed the admiral of the fleet,
another was a moghul lord and brandished yataghan,
                          and yet can these few
so much power bring to bear upon the sword-less folk?
                          And how well they knew
the artless and inflated art of being grand! Cold sneer,
                          sadistic laugh complete
with blackened teeth, a scar, a stare of maddened haughty ice
                          that can browbeat
the trodden folk. And these alone mark out these grander men
                          whose greatness
draws on their disdainful look and looks not at the plainness
                          of their fateless,
surly self that lives in the now and builds our hell on earth:
removes our plenty and leaves a land of dearth.

"Here are my brothers," the wise man sang,
                          and grinned in Dionysian glee,
"I have lauded all your lordly deeds and more, and asked no fee,"
he servile nodded to their bloated selves, "except your pleasure."
He kissed the chief man's hand: "Your victories are my treasure!"
"You're right," the potentate pronounced while swinging high
                          his scimitar to catch pure light,
to form the figure of the strong, to carve his name
                          on centuries long
with epic deeds of those who kill not for vengeance but for thrill
of wilful strength that idles – erratic and fanatic, unreasoned

and unseasoned by the conscious; thus inhuman in its fatal,
                  fateful will to be
the thing that is and cannot see the weakness of the wilful state
                  that hears no plea
of compassion

And down it came and severed air and rived the wise man's
                  head of hair.
"Goodbye, old man, you served us well; I speed you on the road
                  to hell
so you can Dionysian dance the well-marked way your
                  well-intended stance
marked out while spinning your words to serve us killers
                  of contempted herds.
His father was a priest, a dogmat of the Christian cult
                  who straight-backed walked
amongst the herd and joyless confirmed them
                  in their herdish ways and talked
the talk of life to come and hopes eternal beyond the
                  fierceness of our rule.
He stole their bodies and he stole their souls;
                  the coarseness of his school
left little hope of living life up to its brim and going beyond
                  the petty part the pawn
plays in my hands," the chief man roared, while wiping blood
                  from the sword he'd drawn
light-heartedly. "But what of him, the son who came from those
                  he loved to scorn?"
"He served us well with all his intellectual force and traitored those
                  who work upon the hill –

and set off on his ineffectual course to go beyond while doing ill
to those for whom he should have cared.
                        As one of us he could not be:
we do no thinking in our bold equestrian crowd.
Proudly we get others to do that paltry thing,
as others do our digging, forests cut
and fill our coffers with their well-gotten gains:
do they not see how we can govern
and leave so little for their enduring pains?"

I wept and kept my distance from their jocund and unruffled
                        wrath;
I buried genius in the sands after placing his spear in both hands;
I prayed to God for the godless seer
                        and longed for a time when he could appear
harmless for his bold falsehoods. Dust denoted
                        the diminution of the brutal behemoth
That he so loved.

Fascism encountered in a city park

The black dog ran, and leather, close-cropped man
youthful followed on behind,
on his unbending course he cut a wash
of women pushing prams and silent boys
who watched and wondered whether
future growth would grow to hollow
strength such as the weak admire
when pulling on the grand attire
of weekend warriors who can only follow.

Gut fear and fury felt within a quicker heart,
I circled round his arrowed path and fled.
The day is young, he cannot harm;
the day is old, he has his charm,
misplaced perhaps, but can I pose
the problem now the park gates close.

The well-drop drew ...

The well-drop drew the clattered sound of empty pail,
but drew no hope of things to come
that are not hardened forms of needless needs.
The battered tin, the droughted well,
the weather-cock that foolish spins
upon the spindle of the spire, lifted high
by the house of God, whose windows
rattle in the soulless breeze.

In you who believe in nothing else,
I found the thing we cannot find within ourselves,
in these empty times of packaged thought,
feelings folded in coloured cards, and endless objects
squeezed into the grinning adman's gawdy box.
While sound-bites swallow with voracious speed,
this empty land, a blade of grass, and you, my creed.

**You are either with us or against us
in the clash of civilizations**

>These are the men of the gallows cold,
>bold men they kill, and still return
>and swarm and swear
>allegiance to all order
>that rigid regulates the soul
>and calls it freedom.
>
>And how they hoard historic things,
>distort the rope of the past,
>and make a noose of harsh ideas.
>They march within us all,
>these men of steel,
>cast them out
>and then begin to feel
>the sameness that makes us human.

The Moment

This all is nothing, and this nothing
all beauty contains within its momentary flash.
The swallow swoops and flings its sinewed self
into the downward flight – and feels, for feel it must,
as wind bathes it in the coolest rush across unmeasured
metric grids which are measured by my heart.

This private moment comments on the fraying senses of my self,
the rush of time and all its integers banal and beautiful
that stack themselves upon the onward course I can conceive
but fleetingly. I no longer have the innocence to feel,
nor have I gained the wisdom to know and understand.
I linger and the turmoil of this world slips from my hand.
Only this empty moment which I spectate is in my clasp;
amongst this fractured stillness, something knowable
comes close and just eludes the closing fingers of my mind's grasp.

Prayer to the muse

Of what could all this lively world consist,
if not our well-intended intents to
fulfil ourselves in all we say and do?
Let these attempts to let my passions rip
fulfil ambitions of my clouded brain
which bring such sweetness to a life of pain
and plain monotone.

A joyous solitude

I rose and raised the life in me
to catch the sharpened light that cut the sea
with morning's contrasts bright and shadowed gloom,
ecstatic voice that called and played a tune
upon the tautened strings of my fibred room
that is my fleshy sensored self, my living
tomb of separatedness planted in this most green-bogged
land of silences that cling and elusive sounds.
I sigh, delightful joy I feel in feeling for the bounds
of water which must hem me in with sweet geometry
of bays and headland mounds – more rigid, limpid,
honest too, than all the cages of our human zoo.

Songs of Europe

I canti d'Europa

Europe

Europe, what is your race?
  The race of all who have no race.
Europe, what is your creed?
  The creedless creed of those who want to think.
Europe, what is your tongue?
  The tongue that proudly speaks its unique song
  of difference, and does not plunge into the wordless
  narrows of commercial speak and speechless emptiness.
Europe, what are your dreams?
  The dream that Europe shall shape itself, and leave off
  shaping other folks. The dream that doesn't dream too much,
  and makes a friend of all who have a dream to share.
  The dream that all will have respect and peaceful live
  in ignorance of what it is to fight.
Europe, what do you think of this?
  I wish that it were so.

Europa

Europa, vecchia sgualdrina,
porto dei popoli che chiude le porte,
chi vorrebbe sdraiarsi con te?
E sentire il tuo odor di razzismo,
quell'alito cattivo di vanti marciti
e quel gobbo gobinesco che porti
così fieramente, come se fosse
il seno di ragazza serena.

Vecchia sgualdrina,
ti sei mai guardata nello specchio?
Serva e signora, hai tante pretese
ma altro non sai far che seguir il potente,
e affogar i poveri che ti vengon incontro.
Vecchia sgualdrina, tu puzzi di muffa,
ti abbandoniamo, continente, nel tuo letto incontinente.

[Europe, you old whore, / haven for peoples that is shutting its doors, / who would want to lie with you? / And smell your smell of racism, / that bad breath of putrefied boasts and that Gobinesque hunchback that you flaunt so proudly, as though it were / the breast of an untroubled young woman. // You old whore, / have you never looked at yourself in the mirror? / Both servant and lady, you have so many pretensions, / but you only know how to follow the powerful, / and to drown the poor people who come to meet you. / You old whore, you smell of mould, / we leave you, continent, to your incontinent bed.]

Europe, my love

Europe, my love, your eyes like polished stones
look out on distant worlds and welcomes smile to ages
of their comings. "I am you," you say,
"and if you do not come, then I will die
or shrivel." Your loving lips cry out,
and generous limbs fly on along the rubbled ground,
and up you lift the flag the free, fraternal and equal
follow, while beyond the barricade, the troubled sound
of those who cannot know their action's sequel.

Europe, my love, your dark eyes sparkle.
And we would willing lie in your embrace
of hopeless hopes. How many dreams
have you unloaded on an overloaded world?
You care little, little did you esteem
how we, the heirs to your ambitious folly,
would wither in your unattainable scheme.

Europe, you killed ...

Europe, you killed your Jews, cut out
transnational heart, expelled the best,
most civil self you had, and sent it out
to be a caricature of yourself, lest
you should pay your crime, and it became
a people who could hate and hate
the shadows of what they used to be.

Europe, you killed your Gypsy soul,
and banned dark smiles of lively will.
And meanly distrust them still.
To east and west to some degree,
you have no room for them to be
themselves and Europe's children too.

Italian poems

Le poesie italiane

La letteratura

Dir udirò di lontani scogli,
travagli sentirò di intime voglie;
racconta di continuo quel letterato
convinto, gira e rigira e l'amor e'l fato.
Proclama e declama l'utopico stato,
prova e disprova l'ultimo significato
di questa e quell'altra vita.

Lo sento, lo seguo,
lo s'impara, lo si cita.
Ho messo le mani nell'intreccio del suono,
ho intriso le dita nell'intrico dell'uomo
e delle donnesche esistenze.
Ho perso il punto dove tutto s'annoda.
Credenze, sentenze, esperienze,
succube sarò di quelle alla moda.

(Literal translation: *Literature*. I will hear tell of distant rocky shores, I will hear tell of intimate desires; that earnest man of letters is continuously telling stories, giving various takes on love and fate. He proclaims and declaims the utopian state, proves and disproves the ultimate meaning of this life and the next. I hear him and I follow him, we learn from him and we quote him. I have put my hands in the web of words and have soaked my fingers in the intricacies of man and female existences. I have lost the point where it all comes together. Beliefs, aphorisms, experiences: I will be a slave to the ones that are in fashion.)

Sotto la statale

Nel cuore della calma,

morbida s'estende

l'aria offuscata attraverso la valle.

Chiazze di nebbia

s'avvinghiano agli alberi, ai cespugli.

La luce fioca del mattino

desta il verde pastello dal sonno;

sonnolenza s'appiccica alla mia esistenza,

dileguo nel corpo sfumato della terra.

Lunghe arterie, viottoli sterrati bordati d'arbusti

mi portano il sostegno

dell'anima materna della terra.

Fra un'ora scoccherà

di là sul ciglio della collina

dove passa la statale

il frastuono dei chilometri orari

dove prima tutta la distesa serbava il tempo intero.

(*Below the State Road*: In the heart of tranquillity, the soft, darkened air stretches across the valley. Patches of fog cling to trees and bushes. The weak morning light wakes the pastel green from its sleep; sleepiness clings to my existence and I dissolve into the faded body of the earth. Long arteries, dirt tracks bordered with shrubs, bring me the support of the earth's maternal soul. In an hour's time, the noise of kilometres-per-hour will be triggered on the ridge of the hill where the state road passes – where previously the whole expanse contained all time itself.)

Se oggi il sole non splende, non usi lo sciampo migliore

    Pura fantasia

    può riempir il vuoto

    dell'ambizione

    di acquisire tanto

    più

    più di ogni altro.

    Più cresce l'ambizione

    più che devono soffrire,

    più ci si perde nel sogno

    di avere sempre di più.

    Il braccio secco e la pancia gonfia

    sono lontani.

    La miseria ha due dimensioni sui fogli dei giornali.

    Più reali sono i giovani sorridenti;

    i loro visi – maschere di salute;

    corrono sulla spiaggia

    e bevono Coca-Cola.

(*If the sun isn't shining today, you are not using the right shampoo*: Pure fantasy can fill the vacuum left by the ambition to acquire so much more than anyone else. The more ambition grows, the more they have to suffer, the more we lose ourselves in the dream of always having more. The thin arms and swollen stomachs are far off. Poverty has two dimensions on the pages of a newspaper. More real are the smiling youths. Their faces are masks of health. They run along the beach and drink Coca-Cola.)

Quelle sere

Non più
sento l'aria afosa della sera
sudore ma men del mattino
che s'affaticava nella canicola
crudele.
Che riposo, quelle sere calde
dopo giorni ancor più caldi,
crudeli,
perché sotto quel sole
un bambino gridava,
la fame faceva come una palla
la sua pancia gonfia.

Non più
sento le belle sensazioni
di quelle sere bengalesi
che celavano
la rabbia dei rubati.
Espropriata
anche la vita
sfruttata da altre classi
e da altri paesi.
Il crepuscolo copriva il senso di colpa.

La sera si riposava,
comoda come l'occidente
che si scorda dell'oriente
tranne quando riscuote i tributi
della miseria.

(*Those evenings*: I no longer feel the stifling air of the evening; sweat but less than the morning that laboured through the cruel dog day. What relief those hot evenings brought after even hotter, crueller days, because under that sun a child cried out, and the hunger had turned his stomach into a ball. No longer do I feel the wonderful sensations of those Bengali evenings that hid the anger of the victims of theft. Even life had been expropriated by other classes and other countries. The dusk assuaged the sense of guilt. The evening took a rest, comfortable like the West which forgets the East except when it collects the tributes of destitution.)

L'uomo solitario

L'uomo, costretto a parlar con sé,
l'orme nella neve calca,
continua, sotto'l sole fioco,
fiacco a borbottar.
Scioglie in lui un estro
esterrefatto; a noi
non importa più
lo sgelo d'un discorso
detto fra denti stretti,
condensa nell'aria,
fumo,
e sul bianco ci dipartimmo.

(The man, obliged to talk to himself, pressed his footprints into the snow, and continued under the weak sun to mutter wearily. A bewildered eccentricity thawed and broke free within him; we no longer care about the thaw of a discourse spoken through gritted teeth, condensation in the air, smoke, and across the whitened ground we went our separate ways.)

Una donna

La bambina
nata sorridente
giocando bene al sogno,
cresceva:
divenne donna
sposata.
Attrasse intorno
un brulicar di cose
lavabili,
da mettere a posto;
ore pulite con l'aiax
l'allontanavano da sé.

Nacquero i bambini
che strappavano i giorni,
cantò
ma sentì la sua voce lontana
spersa fra le strilla.

(The little girl was born laughing, and playing well with the dream she grew: she became a woman – a married woman. She drew around her a swarm of things that can be washed and tidied away; hours cleaned with Ajax took her away from herself. The children were born and they tore away the days; she sang but she heard her voice as distant and lost amongst the screams.)

Come dobbiamo pesare ...

Come dobbiamo pesare
chi pesa le parole?
colui che scolpisce
il suon del significato,
e pien di calore umano
canta da solo -
cuor gelido.

Cammina sui ciottoli
smussati dai carri
carichi di lavoro,
non sente il sudore
ma segue i solchi
nella pietra,
affascinato dal roteare
di tante ruote
e di tanti anni.

Acqua schiumosa di sapone
scende la scanalatura.
Il sol lo secca,
cambia la tonalità del grigio.

(How should we weigh up the person who weighs up words? – the person who sculpts the sound of meaning full of human warmth, but sings on his own with a cold heart? He walks on a cobbled street worn down by carts loaded with work; he does not feel the sweated labour but follows the ruts in the cobbles, fascinated by the turning of so many wheels over so many years. Water frothy with soap runs down the groove, and the tone of grey changes.)

In cerca del canto

Ho visto anch'io queste colline
curve sul piano, crine
di cipressi, miei i sogni
d'appartenere
a quella campagna in bonaccia,
cascine lontane
canto di mulinello
mente che macina memorie
rifatte,
canto che consola.

Egli nel mondo almanaccato
con sforzo di fantasia
un sorriso divertito
lanciava.
Beato in sé stava
ed io, lacrimando,
costruivo statue di neve
sciolte dallo sguardo di lui.

Passarono di qua i carri stranieri
ruvidi ricordi d'una mente stravolta.
Il cigolio d'un peso che non corre;
accenti inusitati cadevano come brina
sulla terra gelida,
un grido d'aiuto che non sento.

Rimango in me
in cerca del canto
né lui né lei
li guardo in faccia
mi sdraio sull'erba
non rinuncio all'inutile caccia.

(*In search of a song*: I too have seen the hills curving down to the plain, horsehair of cypress trees and my dreams of belonging to that becalmed countryside, distant farmhouses, whirlwind song, a mind that mills rehashed memories, a song that consoles. He, in this dreamt-up world and forcing his fantasy, let fly an amused smile. He was happy in himself and I, tearful, built statues of snow that he melted with his stare. The foreign tanks came by this way, coarse memories of a convulsed brain. The metallic sound of a weight that cannot rush; uncommon accents fell like frost upon the frozen ground, a cry of help that I cannot hear. I remain within myself still looking for this song, I can look neither him nor her in the face, I lie down on the earth and will not give up my pointless hunt for the song.)

La torre d'avorio

Precondizione

Preconcetto

Preconizzare

Propongo

Proposizione

Pare

che lui, sorriso in bocca

bastone in mano,

menasse,

crudelmente trucidasse.

Non so,

penso per me.

Faccio collezione di parole,

farfalle preziose,

trafitte da spilloni;

valgono più d'ogni emozione.

Sono condizionato.

(*The ivory tower.* Precondition, preconception, to predict, I propose, affirmation, it appears that he, with a smile on his lips and a cudgel in his hand, beat people up and cruelly slaughtered. I don't know; I mind my own business. I make a collection of words, precious butterflies pierced by a pin; they are worth more than any emotion. I am conditioned.)

Il riflusso

I nidi si rivelarono nodi
nell'intreccio dei rami,
il vento si fece freddo,
ed io, intimo essere (egoista),
di me curando
cercavo il letargo.
Quel sonno lungo, senza sensi.

(*The downturn in our political consciousness* [my apologies – the translation of poetry can be hellish – the word *riflusso* can also be translated as the 'ebb tide', but was widely used in the sense given here during the eighties]: The nest proved to be knots amongst the interweaving branches, the wind has turned cold, and I, an intimate and selfish being caring only for myself, sought out hibernation/ lethargy/ torpor. That long sleep without feelings.)

Ancora riflusso

Devono disfare tutto, perchè tutto
rifatto da noi dovrà essere.
Un lavoro di Penelope
dove debolezza è la forza
della nostra ragione, e il ricordo
la nostra arma.

Lasciamoli sghignazzar,
sono nati per rifar
l'orgoglio materiale;
sono nati per non essere.

(*The downturn again*: They have to undo everything, so that everything will have to be remade by us again. A job for Penelope, in which weakness is the strength of our reason, and memory our weapon. We should leave them to laugh contemptuously; they were born to reconstruct pride in material wealth, they were born for a non-existence.)

A touch of myopia

I hold within my mind all those I've loved;
but how they fade and travel far along
the sweetened thread of what could have been.

Words unsaid, and too many words cascading
with the hurtful force of doubts about what really was
and now is only clicking in my head. A vantage lost,
a touch no longer felt, a kindness forgotten in the rush,
and all, all so sudden, slips away and wanly smiles.

Was it good or bad? Did I do wrong, or was I
wronged a little, but not too much within this world
of horrors deep and tragic acts unknown to me.
I smile and feel the strength of having been
a lucky man who met much good and slithered past
the dogs who rule and those who don't, but try their best.